TAKECONOMICS:

A Counterintuitive Perspective

Brooks Robinson

Copyright
©Brooks B. Robinson
ISBN: 9781096099796
BlackEconomics.org
<u>www.BlackEconomics.org</u>
P.O. Box 8848
Honolulu, Hawaii 96830-8848
September 2018
Essays

Dedication

To Clonzie Brooks and Sallie Robinson Hodge, who helped raise me. To Sister Lee Wilson, who saved my life. To Wylma C.S. Robinson, who helped make my life.

Table of Contents

Preface iv
Introduction 1
Economics and Takeconomics 5
Religion and Takeconomics 7
Business and Takeconomics 10
Black American Operationalization of Takeconomics 15
    Mental/psychological 15
    Physical 15
    Spiritual 18
Epilogue 20

Preface

The devil is a liar, thief, and a murderer!!!

It could be that late in life my mind has chosen to invert reality and has imagined a distorted reality: good versus evil.

It is more likely that age has crystalized insightful wisdom that enables a vision of the world as it really exists.

How does the world exist? A world of haves and have-nots. That is an insight that I have had for very long. What is new here is my comprehension of why this world exists as it does. It is largely the result of mindset—our view of the world because of what we have been permitted to see, hear, and perceive.

Think about it: There are nearly seven and one-half billion people on the planet. Everyone cannot live like a king—at least materially. Therefore, those who have control of resources have wisely chosen to establish a system over the years in which 99 percent of the world is taught to perceive life possibilities from a distorted and constrained perspective.

The formulation of a capitalist-type economic system by Adam Smith during the 18th century and the promulgation of his two key scholarly works (*The Theory of Moral Sentiments* and *The Wealth of Nations*), which espouse individuals working freely to achieve preferred outcomes (the "invisible hand") while acting in a moral Christian context, laid the foundation for the world as we know it today. Still in the 21st century, the world is under the myth and spell that, if you work hard and smart, are thrifty, and do the right thing, then you will experience a materially favorable life.

The argument is buttressed robustly by the idea that the world has scarce resources; hence the study of economics—the so-called study of the distribution of scarce resources.

This series of short essays supplants this understanding of how and why the world's systems have evolved and operate the way that they do. It will be disruptive because, with more and more clamoring for material and wealth elevation, it is very difficult to maintain the status quo.

The objective is to be disruptive and to upset the status quo. The intent is to reset the scene, the premise, and the foundation on which the system stands. Only then can we all consider a "new system of things" in which everyone has a clear view of how the system should really work. To the extent that this new system is understood generally, then the world can reshape itself into a new reality.

Unlike Adam Smith, we do not guarantee that by everyone operating in their own best interest, everyone will be better off—as opposed to some power exercising overarching control of all or certain aspects of the system. Rather, we believe and argue that, in this world, you must make informed choices of how to exert your own power and resources, and how to align with others to achieve the best possible outcome. The key point is that there are no guaranteed outcomes: Temporally, there can be favorable or unfavorable outcomes.

But is not that almost everyone's experience in this life. It is only the well and long-endowed very rich and famous who are guaranteed positive outcomes from generation-to-generation.

So maybe *Takeconomics* is not as "disruptive" as we first imagined. Just recognition of reality.

In any event, we invite you to take time to learn what Takeconomics means for you and yours.

It is coming!

Introduction

What is Takeconomics?

It is the natural order of things. It is what we find in creation.

The creation was, and is, abundant. We are fortunate to come to life in this creation. However, we have needs: Food, clothing, and shelter. That is why we can find freely available in creation food plants and fruit and nut trees; meat animals that can also provide fur for clothing; and building materials with which to produce shelter. In the beginning, and still today in certain places, all of this is free for the taking—hence Takeconomics. There was and is no need to give anything in exchange for these goods—except for the labor required to take them.

Also, there were and are fish in streams, rivers and the seas. However, when the fish supply is reduced, we learn to fish by placing a bit of bait on a hook and line; thereby learning to give a little something in exchange for fish. This need to give a little something for more in return is also evidenced in the pump priming of a well. You pour a little water in through the pump, and it can elicit a flood of water from the well. Planting seeds and harvesting is another prime example of giving a little to obtain much (sowing and reaping). It is important to note that in none of these cases is the item given to get much produced by man. The bait, the water, and seed are all natural in the creation.

Therefore, the natural world is one of taking what is needed; and if that doesn't work, then giving a little to get what is needed. Because one is taking more than giving in all of these cases, we label it "Takeconomics"—the study of taking resources.

One can argue that the evolution of laws, property rights, and growth of the global population necessitated economizing because scarcity arose; i.e., these developments legitimized use of the word "economics." However, even in today's world of nearly seven and one-half billion humans, there still is considerable open space that is not effectively controlled or managed. This means that Takeconomics can still apply.

Takeconomics is acceptable when practiced in the context of creation. It goes somewhat awry when humans are treated as elements of creation—to be taken freely or by offering a little.

On the other hand, even in our information, computer, and digital world, Takeconomics can work with humans. However, the humans should be fully knowledgeable concerning the principles of Takeconomics; comprehends life's possibilities under such a system; and be free to operationalize their choices under the system.

One should be willing to accept a Takeconomics system as long as one is prepared to take from creation what is required; or to engage in the beneficial practice of giving something in exchange for more. The first clause is self-explanatory; the second clause requires some explication. Namely, that the second principle of Takeconomics should prevail—giving something and getting more in return

A problem with our current social system is that it is structured so that most of the agents in the system do not receive a multifold return in response to their giving. Yes, it is true that farmers are not guaranteed bumper crops each year. But, for the most part, poor crops are the exception—otherwise farmers exit farming. However, for most workers in the social system, they work a lifetime with little chance of even dying in the black. This is inconsistent with Takeconomics. Again, over and over again, the creation is paused to give us what we need freely, or to give us much by simply taking some small amount from creation to use in the production of much.

Takeconomics is a well-designed system. It is the system of creation. But it is not working for the entire human population. Those who are the entrenched wealthy have evolved a hybrid Takeconomic system (capitalism), which works well for them, but not for most of the population. This leads to a logical question: How can we return Takeconomics to truly functional operations?

An answer is that we should move away from glutinous materialism and wealth hording. Not to "economize," but to realize that the body can only consume one meal at a time, and that one should consume the proper food. We must realize that we can only wear one set of clothes at a time. And we should realize that we can only be in one room at a time. Therefore, while needs should be met fully, **there should be a moratorium on excess.** The animals in creation do not generally exhibit excessive behavior.

In its purest form, Takeconomics works, and, arguably, most humans would be happy living in such a system when it is operationalized properly. Therefore, one can argue that the unhappiness, psychosis, depression, and related ailments present in the current system are a consequence of trying to function in a capitalist (i.e., non-Takeconomics) environment.

"Free-market capitalism," never worked, and was never designed to work, for all. Theoretically, free-market capitalism is based on the individual; however, those who have been successful in the system have never operated individually. Rather, they have banded together under corporate business arrangements to generate wealth and success for themselves and their posterity.[1] Those who were, and are, among the uninitiated to free-market

---

[1] A key aspect of the debate about our current commercial/financial system is the role of large corporations: Apple, Amazon, Facebook, Google, Walmart, Wells Fargo, etc. These corporations wield great power and determine numerous social outcomes. While the uninformed may believe that these corporations benefit a wide swatch of the population through share ownership, the reality is that less than 40 percent of corporate shares are owned by Households and Nonprofit Institutions (see the US Federal Reserve Board's *Financial Accounts of the United States* for 2017, March 20, 2018). For more on the power wielded by large corporations, see David McLaughlin (2018), "Are US Companies Too Big and Powerful? The FED Wants to Know," Bloomberg, August 22.

capitalism and accept it at face value tread the system alone. This left and leaves them vulnerable to those who band together under cooperative arrangements. Even today, small sole proprietorships can only hope to initiate a successful enterprise. As soon as the enterprise becomes profitable and captures the attention of corporations, in swoops the latter to absorb the former so that the corporation benefits on a large scale. As for those who are not fortunate enough to initiate an individual enterprise, but who offer their labor to enterprises, they stand at the mercy of the haves and remain have-nots.

The hoggish and lying controllers of the system repeatedly devise concepts and principles, promulgate these concepts and principles to the unknowing majority, but practice the exact opposite concepts and principles themselves. As a result, the controllers keep most in the society deaf, dumb, and blind to how the system works (Takeconomics). If one is fortunate enough to think counterintuitively and decipher the system, but is not prepared to conform completely, then that one's life is at stake. If one who deciphers the system chooses to conform, then a meager payoff is extended—crumbs from the rich man's table. What else should one expect when those in control have the power?

Takeconomics is different. It clarifies the basic principles of taking from the creation to produce to meet needs. Like the creation, it requires aligning oneself cooperatively with a community (not standalone individuals) to participate in collaborative production as required to meet needs. When Takeconomics is operationalized properly and fairly, all of those who participate in collaborative production have a voice in what is produced and how the production is dispensed.

Economics and Takeconomics

It is common knowledge that "economics" is "the study of the distribution of scarce resources." But have you ever questioned why the resources are scarce for particular groups of people and not for others? More importantly, have you ever asked why we never seem to run out of food or oil?

In the former case, it seems legitimate that the definition of economics should say that it is: "the study of the distribution of scarce resources for non-White people of the world." Why? Because the White world is not typically faced with scarce resources. If certain Whites in the world face scarcity, then the main reason for this is because that group of Whites has distanced itself from the body politique of the White or European Western world writ large. The White outgroup can resolve this issue by simply reliving the "prodigal son" story and coming into alignment with the larger group's requirements.

When we say the White world is devoid of scarcity, clearly, we do not intend that the Western world's streets are paved with gold, or that milk and honey flow through the streets. What is intended is that the Western White world has plenty of food, clothes, shelter, transportation, education, healthcare, entertainment, etc. On the other hand, in the non-White world, there are innumerable cases where Black, Brown, Red, and Yellow people are without.

When discussing no dearth of food or oil—and we are talking mainly of the White or Western world—we know about the Green Revolution of the 1960s and about fracking of the 21st century. It seems that the White world continues to find ways to produce and find more of whatever is required. And even if the world consumes its last drop of oil, the world is already well on its way to meeting energy needs using so many other methods: nuclear, solar, wind, hydro, and hydrogen. As for food, we are already well down the path to producing more food through bio-engineering and/or by developing foods through synthetic processes.

So, where's the scarcity?

If there is no scarcity in the White or European world, then the term "economics" does not apply. The term may have applied at some point in the past. But in the 21st century, the term does not apply. What term applies to the White or European World system? Takeconomics.

To whom does the term "economics" apply? To the Non-White people of the world. Why do Black people face scarcity? Because we allow the White or European world to engage in Takeconomics, while we are convinced that we must engage in economics—living with scarcity.

When you live under Takeconomics, you simple ensure that you take more than you give. On the other hand, if you live under an economics regime, then you economize to make ends meet. After the White world takes hoggishly what it desires, the Black world is forced to economize.

To this very day, the White/Western world is practicing Takeconomics in the Black world; taking very valuable material and human resources, and forcing the Black world to economize.[2]

All of this tells us that the White and Black worlds are different—especially when it comes to the systems that are in place to manage the development, production, and distribution of resources, goods, and services.

Obviously, this difference exists between the United States and Europe versus Africa and, to a lesser extent, Asia. But the difference also exists between White and Black ethnic groups within the United States and elsewhere in the Americas. Clearly, the question to ask is: "What is there to be done about this difference?"

---

[2] A highly prized future text will be a volume that catalogues across human history the value of material and human resources that have been extracted and exported out of Africa and the rest of the non-White world to the Western world. As you know, the Western world has fueled, and continues to support, its development significantly using untold resources from the non-White world.

Religion and Takeconomics

We are not religious scholars; therefore, we will not seek to explore this topic in great depth. Why do we bring religion into this discussion of resources, production, and consumption? The reasoning is that any Christian—and most of the Black world is Christian or a derivative thereof—knows the *Genesis* story. The story goes that God placed man and woman in the "Garden of Eden," making literally everything available to them for the taking—including knowledge of good and evil. The point being, there was no need for man to engage in production. Everything was available free of charge and with little work effort. This is a Takeconomics system at it best.

The *Genesis* also says that God gave humans dominion over the creation—the land, herbs, trees, seas, animals, birds, sky, fish, mountains, and valleys—everything.

When reading a work, one can stop at any point in the process, and one can interpret what is written as one chooses. Our view of what the White world has done with respect to the *Genesis* is to read it in all of its positive potential for man: Control of all earthly things and free access to satisfy wants. In addition, those in the White world concluded that they were made in God's image (White), and in his son's image (Jesus). This is consistent with a people who constructed a book for themselves and others simultaneously as a basis for a White Supremacy system.

On the other hand, Black people of the world were taught about their sinful nature (the Hamitic curse), which meant that they should preoccupy themselves with performing penance throughout history to get back to a state of grace where they too could claim the right to control the earth and its resources and to consume freely to satisfy needs. In part, that is why many Black people still today operate under the Hamitic curse and hate their Black selves. They have self-hate because they are convinced that they are sinful flesh, are not vicegerents of creation, and cannot consume freely the produce and fat of the land.

Therefore, while the White world operates as vicegerents of the creation and enjoys the associated bounties, the Black world is happy just to be alive and barely surviving in a world with riches beyond measure. Whites practice Takeconomics. Blacks practice economics.

To restore balance to the world, Black people must recognize the inversion of the *Genesis* myth, read it from a positive perspective, rise to the level of vicegerents of creation, and be beneficiaries of the mercy, graciousness, and plentifullness of God and his creation. Let us take from *Genesis* and the *Holy Bible* that which will be beneficial and leave the rest alone. In fact, as we have argued elsewhere, Black people of the world should re-realize our own original religion that placed us in the aforementioned favorable roles.[3] It is only by doing so that we can transform a world and life of *samsara* into a world and life of joy.

The primary hurdle for the Black world is turning the White world away from its Takeconomics when it comes to areas of the world dominated by us. Let us stop the White world, which displays an insatiable appetite, from practicing Takeconomics with our natural and human resources and markets. Having done that, we must then learn to use our resources and markets for our benefit—learning to practice Takeconomics in a non-glutinous manner.

We need to embrace our old religion and accompany it with an old but rejuvenated social system. The old religion will teach that we have every right to have nonexcessive wants and desires; to work collaboratively and faithfully to meet those wants and desires; and to experience good and success all around.

But we should be wiser than the Western/White world, which had a ravenous and unconstrained thirst for materialism. We should formalize a religious and social system that teaches true harmony with the creation so that we can enjoy the benefits of the creation forever. We know and have seen the creation's ability to

---

[3] See Brooks Robinson (2010), *Change: Black America's Religion*, BlackEconomics.org. Honolulu, Hawaii.

regenerate itself if given sufficient time to do so. Therefore, we should practice intelligent Takeconomics that permits us to satisfy our needs in a plentiful—not hoggish—manner, while allowing the Earth to restore what we take from it.

Most importantly, we should start yesterday. A key question is whether we have sufficient time to restore a planet that has been nearly destroyed by a selfish mind bent on materialism? Let us tell it like it is: The White materialistic mind was and is focused only on creating material wealth, with little-to-no concern about the impact on Mother Earth and the remainder of its people. The argument is that, through materialism (including robotization, artificial intelligence, information technology, and other sciences), the means to restore the Earth will be identified. Given the history of the world, it is unlikely that the White mind will devote resources sufficient to save anyone or anything other than itself—unless one is willing to pay dearly.[4] Again, the White world may "take" the liberty to try to seek to restore its part, the poorer part of the Earth, and leave our part, the better part of the Earth, to collapse. What the White mind does not seem to recognize is that God, Creation, and Man are all one. You cannot save a portion without saving the whole.

In the end, we can rest assured that Takeconomics is the correct mindset and course of action. Otherwise, how could He say: "Ask and it shall be given, seek and ye shall find, knock and it shall be open unto you" (*Holy Bible*, Matthew 7:7). It must all be here already for the taking. And it is!

---

[4]Readers may conclude that there is a countervailing argument and submit the 2015 Paris Agreement and the United Nations Framework Convention on Climate Change as evidence. We argue that the Agreement fails to rationalize why the so-called developing world should pay one cent for cleaning up the Earth that has been made nearly uninhabitable over the past 130 years by the Western World. The latter invented the combustion engine and other devices that are primary sources of greenhouse gases—the cause of climate change. Notably, the US intends to withdraw from the Agreement, and, potentially, use its annual $3 billion contribution to build a more robust space program—a place to survive when the Earth fails.

Business and Takeconomics

It is probably best to begin at the beginning. In the creation, as we know it, animals that go it alone do not generally wield extraordinary power. Rather, animals that form associations seem to fare much better; i.e., they can defend themselves and obtain nutrition successfully. Of course, this does not mean that associative relationships come without internal strife. However, nature has designed a mechanism that permits internal conflict to be resolved within the associative relationship, and the larger group can be preserved and continue advancing. Thus, down through the ages have come lions, tigers, elephants, and even wolves, as examples of animals who associate in groups to survive—and even thrive.

It is therefore instructive for one intent on doing business to take note. Once upon a time, it was possible to initiate a single enterprise, and to preserve it as an entity through time. Without amassing support, the carpenter, blacksmith, and farmer could pass the enterprise down through the generations. But the rise of the corporation, equity markets, and the financing that they can produce, has made it increasingly difficult to create and preserve a standalone enterprise.

In the late 19th century when large corporations sought to gain increasing market power by swallowing up small enterprises, antitrust legislation surfaced.[5] It halted the march of corporations for an extended period. But by the end of the 20th century, antitrust efforts lost their footing as the great deregulator (US President Ronald Reagan) spurred a

---

[5] The Sherman Anti-Trust Act, which was passed in 1890, represents key antitrust legislation that slowed the formation of monopolies in the US.

surge of mergers and acquisitions, which increased industries' concentration tremendously.

Today, if you are a brilliant innovator, the best that you can hope for is that you survive for a short period of time to see your innovations blossom. But you must be willing to step aside and permit the great behemoths to suck up your enterprise or suffer the consequences. The great multinational corporations may even reward you handsomely for your efforts. But increasingly, at almost all levels, it is difficult to find small enterprises thriving in the Western world for extended periods.

The large multinational (mega) corporations practice Takeconomics. They take financial capital through share and other financial markets and use that capital to absorb or dissolve competitors. Their uptake of required raw materials is phenomenal; they obtain these resources for little or nothing from the developing world—giving a little to obtain much. They combine raw materials with innovation, which they obtain from scientists, who typically receive a minor share of the produce of their labor. In the end, the corporation generates tremendous profits that support dividend distributions to shareholders, who, in turn, are willing to pay even more for equity in the companies. Hence, a seemingly endless upward spiral of commercial power that begets even more commercial power. This is Takeconomics.

In the 21st century in the United States, small entrepreneurs have not fared nearly as well as corporations. Therefore, it is perplexing why certain so-called leaders of the Black economy keep advocating that Black Americans venture into entrepreneurship using a traditional business form—sole proprietorships. Today, many Black Americans believes that the best course of action is to quit their jobs on corporate or government plantations and to strike out on their own to initiate an enterprise. That is why we find the number of Black enterprises mushrooming.

We have written persistently about the shortcomings of Black enterprises, being certain to cite the statistics.[6] Recently, however, we were motivated to explore the topic of failing Black American businesses (sole proprietorships) by looking at the nature of nonfarm sole proprietorships in general—for all ethnic groups in the US.

The source of our statistical analysis was the Internal Revenue Services' Statistics of Income (SOI) Division. The data can be found at the following Internet address; https://www.irs.gov/statistics/soi-tax-stats-nonfarm-sole-proprietorship-statistics. The SOI Division now reflects source data on sole proprietorships for the past 18 years—from 1998-2015. We intended a parsimonious analysis, gathering data only on: (1) the number of sole proprietorships filing tax returns (with and without net income); and (2) the value of total net income. Given this time series, it is inappropriate to consider the data on an historical price basis—inflation is certainly at work. Therefore, we deflated (removed price change from) the data on net income using the gross domestic product (GDP) deflator (2012=100).[7] After accounting for inflation and

---

[6] See the following documents on the BlackEconomics.org Internet website's "Literature" page (www.BlackEconomics.org): "22 Reasons Why Black Businesses Fail" (2014); "A Reality Check on Afrodescendant Entrepreneurship" (2013); and "What Could Have Been: Macrosimulating the Economic Injury Caused by Desegregation" (2007).

[7] Given that nonfarm sole proprietors are engaged in a very wide range of commercial activities, it seems reasonable to use the GDP deflator to deflate the related net income. The GDP deflator represents changes in prices of the full range of production/expenditure activity in the economy. The GDP deflator is available from the US Department of Commerce's Bureau of Economic Analysis at www.bea.gov.

averaging the net income of all sole proprietorship using the number of firms, we realize that these enterprises have levels of real net income that keep their owners below the poverty line—$12,000-to-$15,000 per year. More surprising, of the 17 period changes accounted for over the 18-year period that the data represent, nine of the years reflect a step-back in average real net income (i.e., there are declines). (See Table 1.)

In other words, it is proven repeatedly by the SOI data that sole proprietorships, on average, produce meager net incomes, and the owners of such businesses will generally find that their real net incomes are likely to decline, as opposed to advance, half of the time as they go through the years.

Of course, this is not the end of the story. That is, we are not convicted to suggest to Black Americans that we should not enter into entrepreneurship. On the contrary. We are motivated to hint to Black American prospective entrepreneurs that sole proprietorships represent the wrong form of business in the 21st century. We leave it to others to perform the type of analysis described above for other business forms. However, one might conclude on a general knowledge basis that it is probably in the best interest of Black Americans to think seriously about engaging in business on a cooperative basis, which can lead to corporate business, which may stand a much better chance of surviving, flourishing, and being more profitable than sole proprietorship businesses.[8]

---

[8] To comprehend more about the important history of cooperative economics for Black Americans, and its future potential benefits, readers are directed to: Jessica Nembhard (2014), *Collective Courage: A History of African American Cooperative Economic Thought and Practice*. Penn State University Press. University Park, Pennsylvania; and to Curtis Haynes and Jessica Nembhard (1999), "Cooperative

Sole proprietorship businesses find it difficult to practice Takeconomics, whereas cooperative forms of business have a much better chance of practicing Takeconomics successfully.

Table 1.—Nonfarm Sole Proprietorship's Real Net Income

Periods	Nonfarm Sole Proprietorships	Real Net Income ($'s 000s)	Real Net Income Per Proprietorship ($'s)	Percentage Changes
1998	17,408,809	268,742,902	15,437	
1999	17,575,643	272,374,423	15,497	0.4%
2000	17,904,731	275,032,725	15,361	-0.9%
2001	18,338,190	272,337,346	14,851	-3.3%
2002	18,925,517	272,847,994	14,417	-2.9%
2003	19,710,079	278,934,804	14,152	-1.8%
2004	20,590,691	292,018,199	14,182	0.2%
2005	21,467,566	308,808,213	14,385	1.4%
2006	22,074,953	308,671,362	13,983	-2.8%
2007	23,122,698	303,311,434	13,117	-6.2%
2008	22,614,483	280,603,796	12,408	-5.4%
2009	22,659,976	257,709,886	11,373	-8.3%
2010	23,003,656	278,537,600	12,108	6.5%
2011	23,426,940	288,089,047	12,297	1.6%
2012	23,553,850	304,895,911	12,945	5.3%
2013	24,074,684	297,003,745	12,337	-4.7%
2014	24,631,831	305,783,837	12,414	0.6%
2015	25,226,245	316,764,071	12,557	1.1%

Economics—A Community Revitalization Strategy," *The Review of Black Political Economy*: Vol 27, No. 1, pp. 47-71.

Black American Operationalization of Takeconomics

When Black Americans decide to operationalize Takeconomics in our lives, it must be a comprehensive undertaking: from adopting a new life mindset (mental/psychological), to our perspective on everyday actions (from responding to racist encounters to pushing forward a commercial going concern—physical), to our expectations about what happens when we step through the final door to this existence (spiritual).

Mental/Psychological

Mentally/Psychologically, we should replace the tendency to ask/beg (the posture of a dog at the foot of its master with its tongue hanging out) and expect gifts with a tenacious drive to take what is required to meet our non-glutinous needs. We should learn to step back momentarily and analyze a situation, determine if there is a real and present legitimate need, survey the landscape and see how and where what is needed is available in open space, and then devise a strategy to take in order to meet the need. If we find that we cannot take freely, then we should determine what minimally should be given in return to satisfy our need. We only need to obtain approval from ourselves. We should discontinue, and reject, passivity, which we have employed for generations. Rather, we should adopt fully an active approach to solving our problems and meeting our needs. We have too many unfavorable examples of what has occurred under a regime of passivity, and "loving our enemies."

Physical

Takeconomics is accompanied by a posture of preservation. A fundamental conundrum for Black Americans has been protection and preservation. We have been stuck in a dichotomy of assuming the nature of a Jesus—loving our enemies and turning the other cheek—as opposed to fighting. If enemies are peaceable, then it might be possible to survive and thrive using the Jesus mentality. However, in a world of liars, thieves, and murderers, it is suicide to live as Jesus lived. We live on a savanna and in a jungle where survival is a sign of one that is the fittest and has the highest intellect. We know that for our own benefit we should associate with those with like-minded interests, who are willing to ban with us to protect our own.

For our well-being and survival, we should anticipate the battles that are likely to arise and prepare ourselves for battle. Some might argue that, generally, we should not seek out opportunities to display violent behavior. However, when a small enemy is likely to grow to become a pernicious and large opponent, then it may be wise to take out that small enemy before it grows into a problem. In any event, we should be willing to fight vigorously and violently in the taking process, and then to preserve what we accumulate—if the meeting of present or future needs is involved.

Our first step in this process is taking control of, protecting, and preserving our areas of influence (markets). This entails developing our own security forces and initiating a patrolling of our areas in a given municipality. Once this is achieved effectively, then we can request that municipal governments stop policing by their forces. This will slow the bloodshed and death that is caused by racist police conflict. Municipalities, if they do not have alternative motives/agendas, should be willing to accept this arrangement because it is cost-saving.

A longer-term strategy (over the next five to ten generations—if the earth survives) is to expand our control and areas of influence (markets) from portions of municipalities to envelop entire municipalities; later counties; and ultimately states.[9] Three generations ago, Hispanic Americans began their push into America. Now, through hard and smart work and by being fruitful and multiplying, they are affixing a vice-grip on large parts of California, Texas, New Mexico, Arizona, and Florida. Why did

---

[9] This strategy is consistent with that espoused by the Nation of Islam under the leadership of the late Elijah Muhammad, and as operationalized partly by The Republic of New Afrika primarily under the leadership of the late Chokwe Lumumba in Hinds County, Mississippi and later as Mayor of Jackson, Mississippi.

we not adopt a similar strategy 60 years ago. Think of the progress that we would have made in gaining material and political power had we been more insightful and purposeful.

In our areas of influence, we should practice the type of cooperative Takeconomics already described—pooling resources and developing sizeable going concerns that are large enough to meet real needs and provide returns sufficient to keep participating members out of poverty. While developing such enterprises, we should also push out existing enterprises that "take a basket full of money to the other side of town every evening when the sun goes down."[10] The Irish, Italians, Germans, Asians, and Hispanics, all do the same thing—keep others out of their areas of influence (markets). If it works for them, then what the more for us.

We should practice Takeconomics among ourselves. However, this will be a favorable and useful Takeconomics. As mainly a self-contained area of influence (market and social system), we can control the speed and process of development. Therefore, we can all agree on the production of food, clothing, and shelter necessary to meet all our non-glutinous needs/requirements. We can produce and circulate our own currency and set our own prices. To the extent necessary, we can offer our excess labor services to the outside world and use the related earnings as foreign exchange to acquire goods or services that might be required. Importantly, we can begin to control the flow of media in our areas of influence so that we are not affected adversely by harmful infotainment that may seek to invade our space.

Over the years, as our areas of influence become stronger and expand, we will undoubtedly encounter opposition—those who want to break us down and exploit us again. The first line of defense is economic warfare—producing, consuming, and keeping our resources within. The second line of defense is to actually engage in physical fighting. Given a strong commercial social system, there is no reason why we should not be able to

---

[10] Paraphrasing Malcolm X from his 1964 speech, "The Ballot or the Bullet."

produce or acquire implements of war that enable us to protect ourselves—at least for a limited war. If a limited war escalates, then we will have to rely on world condemnation as a deterrent to the larger nation deploying advanced weaponry against us.

We should not fear war. We fought and died for America in the Revolutionary War, Civil War, World Wars I and II, the Korean and Vietnam Wars, and the Persian Gulf and Afghanistanian Wars. We would certainly fight to protect our little ones. Why, then, should we not fight and die for ourselves and our generations to come? In the wars to come, we will be fighting not against one another, but for each other. We will be fighting for our true freedom; and not in some forlorn lands, but right in our own backyard.

If we do not awaken and begin to operationalize the physical aspects of Takeconomics and fight to protect and preserve ourselves, then it does not mean that we will be at peace and free of war. Everyday is war and death in America for a people who are deaf, dumb, and blind and who suffer and are destroyed because of a lack of knowledge. Fortunately, today, we have a real choice to awaken, begin to live, and to struggle for freedom: first in our own areas of influence, later in cities and counties, and ultimately, in our own Black state.

Spiritual

Our spirit/soul is our life. Is your spirit/soul/life worth less than that of others? Why should you be in want and unable to meet needs, while others consume much more than is required by taking that which is yours? The latter outcome is an injustice in a normal state of nature. It is even more so an injustice when the one in despair has been taught a counterintuitive plan for life. The creation has much to offer, which precludes you having to live under the rule of economics, while others live under a Takeconomics regime. Now that we know that the world is not really upside down, we, too, can begin to enjoy life under Takeconomics.

Spiritually, a burden is lifted. Expectations change. Life becomes much more livable and joyous. Not to know that "Jesus is mine," but to know that the Master Creator of the Universe did not allow you to arrive in this place to be in want, but that everything that you need is available to you freely or by offering some small existing item in return to meet your needs.

With an uplifted heart and mind, you will think better and more enlightened thoughts. You will be able to teach your descendants this age-old reality. With this re-found knowledge and way of life, there will be fewer reasons to take actions that violate your fundamental intuition and moral conscious. You will be able to remain aligned with the creation and the Creator as they are known. As a result, you will remain at peace with yourself and the world around you.

It is this type of deep peace that allowed you to arrive on this planet full of hope, wonder, and joy. It will allow you to pursue your found purpose in life. It will enable you to achieve comfortably your dreams and desires. It is this same peace that will permit you to walk unencumbered, unashamed, and unafraid through the final door to this life when you decease—knowing that, just as all that was needed was for the taking here, then so shall it be on the other side.

Epilogue

In the course of time, the European came to fully comprehend the treasure that was the Earth. It was, and is, filled to the brim with goods required to meet needs. He became greedy and decided to take beyond his own area of influence (Europe, the poorer part of the Earth). He went to the better part of the Earth (Africa and Asia) and started taking. He realized that a simple inversion of the truth made his scheme as easy as taking candy from a baby. He invented economics. Using a counterintuitive interpretation of reality, he blinded the unsuspecting Yellow, Red, Brown, and Black people of the Earth—teaching them economics. He imposed a life of scarcity on them, while practicing Takeconomics and enjoying riches for himself.

Now, the eyes of the world have become open. It is time that we all practice Takeconomics. The question is whether there are sufficient goods left in the earth to meet all of our needs. For all to enjoy the fruits of the Earth, the European may have to go on a diet, abandon a glutinous appetite, and permit the rest of the world to live without want.

For Black Americans, who reside in an "integrated" social system that facilitates superimposition of superiority by Whites, it is imperative that we perform a mental/psychological, physical, and spiritual transformation so that we can obtain our fair share of this Earth. That includes slowly and methodically assuming control of increasing portions of land—from sections of municipalities, to municipalities in their entirety, to counties, even to states. If we form and maintain a vision for our long-term future and practice Takeconomics effectively, then we can obtain much of what is rightfully ours.

Having operationalized Takeconomics appropriately from a commercial perspective, we will find that we can also invert our thinking about so many other areas of life and realize our true greatness. But as the wise ones will tell us, every journey begins with a first step. In this case, our first step is to practice Takeconomics and to relinquish economics.

Advertisements

The Case for Nation Formation (2016) A collection of seven commentaries that build on Coates' "The Case for Reparations." It is unique because it delineates rationales for a Black American effort to initiate our own new nation. The essays describe why we are prepared and qualified to operate our own nation, and they discuss potential outcomes if we do not make the effort. The social-political-economy is ripe for nation formation efforts. It is up to us to take advantage of this temporary opportunity.

Takeconomics:

A Counterintuitive Perspective

TAKE ECONOMICS

21ˢᵗ Century Protests: A Handbook for Black America (2016) Moves the smaller (Black American) nation beyond a cycle of pain, protests, concessions, and then return to the *status quo* with the larger US nation. The book features 12 economic-related strategies that represent pin-point attacks on a system that allows marginal filtering of Black Americans up the economic hierarchy, while ensuring that over 25 percent of Black Americans remain locked out and without hope for advancement. In a Black Lives Matter era that perpetuates the old pattern of marching in the streets and verbal confrontations, *21ˢᵗ Century Protests* provides a new path that reflects the spirit of the American Revolution and economic tit-for-tat strategies. When properly operationalized, *21ˢᵗ Century Protests* can improve Black America's well-being now and into the future.

TAKECONOMICS:

A Counterintuitive Perspective

Brooks Robinson

BlackEconomics.org
www.BlackEconomics.org
BlackEconomics@BlackEconomics.org

www.ingramcontent.com/pod-product-compliance
Lightning Source LLC
Chambersburg PA
CBHW021858170526
45157CB00006B/2499